Successful CVs
in a week

STEVE MORRIS
GRAHAM WILLCOCKS

Hodder & Stoughton

A MEMBER OF THE HODDER HEADLINE GROUP

Acknowledgement

The authors would like to thank Sue McKoen for her help in researching this book.

Order queries; please contact Bookpoint Ltd, 39 Milton Park, Abingdon, Oxon OX14 4TD. Telephone: (44) 01235 400414, Fax: (44) 01235 400454. Lines are open from 9.00 - 6.00, Monday to Saturday, with a 24 hour message answering service. Email address: orders@bookpoint.co.uk

British Library Cataloguing in Publication Data
A catalogue record for this title is available from The British Library

ISBN 0 340 70543 4

First published 1996
Second edition 1998
Impression number   10 9 8 7 6 5 4
Year   2003 2002 2001 2000

Copyright © 1996, 1998 Steve Morris and Graham Wilcocks

All rights reserved. No part of this publicaiton may be reproduced or transmitted in any form or by any means, electronic or mechanical, including photocopy, recording, or any information storage and retrieval system, without permission in writing from the publisher or under licence from the Copyright Licensing Agency Limited. Further details of such licences (for reprographic reproduction) may be obtained from the Copyright Licensing Agency Limited, of 90 Tottenham Court Road, London W1P 9HE.

Typeset by Multiplex Techniques Ltd, St Mary Cray, Kent
Printed for Hodder & Stoughton Educational, a division of Hodder Headline Plc, 338 Euston Road, London NW1 3BH by Cox & Wyman Ltd, Reading.

the Institute
of Management

The Institute of Management (IM) is the leading organisation for professional management. Its purpose is to promote the art and science of management in every sector and at every level, through research, education, training and development, and representation of members' views on management issues.

This series is commissioned by IM Enterprises Limited, a subsidiary of the Institute of Management, providing commercial services.

Management House,
Cottingham Road,
Corby,
Northants NN17 1TT
Tel: 01536 204222;
Fax: 01536 201651
Website: http://www.inst-mgt.org.uk

Registered in England no 3834492
Registered office: 2 Savoy Court, Strand,
London WC2R 0EZ

C O N T E N T S

Everyone should write a curriculum vitae, a potted history of their life, a CV. However, for many people, writing a CV is a little like reading *War and Peace* – it's something they intend to do one day but not quite yet. For many other people the request for a CV is greeted with a cheery:

I've got one somewhere but it's a bit out of date I'm afraid.

This book will help you take the plunge and write a CV that gets results for you – an interview for a job. You will work step by step throughout the week and at the end you will have a first-rate CV and a covering letter to go with it. All you'll need then is a first class stamp, an envelope, and a dash of good fortune.

The steps you will work through as you write your CV are:

- researching yourself
- researching the company you will send your CV to and deciding whether to apply
- deciding on what CV format to choose depending on your circumstances
- avoiding the basic errors that would spell Do Not Pass Go
- writing the CV itself
- editing and checking it
- writing a professional, sharp and interesting covering letter
- popping everything in the post.

Your week looks like this:

Sunday	Thinking about you
Monday	Getting the basics right
Tuesday	Knowing you...
Wednesday	Knowing me...
Thursday	Getting down to the writing
Friday	Almost there
Saturday	Getting your CV across to the employer

Thinking about you

Today you will do some thinking about why your CV is so important and you'll make a start on putting some relevant information together. Few people approach the task of writing their CV with unbridled joy; in fact for many people it's a chore. For others, it can seem daunting.

Most of us see CVs as a necessary evil: as a way of just getting our foot in the door and getting a face to face interview. It's probably for this reason that people put less thought into CVs than they should. However it does pay to put time into writing your CV – both thinking time and writing and editing time.

Rules, rules, rules

A word about the approach this book takes. The world of CV writers has been bedevilled by silly and arbitrary rules. Pick up three books on CVs and each will advise differently on tiny details – like whether to write a date as 3.4.98 or as 3 April 1998. This may explain why people often say many books on CVs are impossible to read.

This book's approach is deliberately different and is based on respect for the reader. We haven't made up arbitrary rules, because we trust your judgement about what is right for you and we have placed CVs in that context.

Some early thoughts

Before you get on to thinking through your strengths and
weaknesses, it's worth bearing in mind a number of key
thoughts. These will help you focus on why CVs are so
important and some of the work you need to do in the early
stages of putting one together.

> *Ask yourself:*
>
> Why are CVs important... why do they matter at all?

Why CVs are important

Employers want them   Recruitment and selection techniques
have moved on over the years with assessment centres and
psychometric testing. But a vast number of jobs at all levels
still require you to send in the humble CV. Some informal
research for this book revealed that at least 80% of jobs will
require a CV of some kind.

> *Firms ask for a CV because:*
>
> • It's a way of giving you a chance to present yourself
>   in your own way
> • It saves them having to draw up an effective form
> • Keeping CVs on file for months or years saves time
>   and money, when they go back through them before
>   advertising a vacancy in the press.

This means that you need to anticipate your CV having a
reasonably long shelf-life.

They're a foot in the door   You won't get that job without an interview, and you won't get the interview without a successful CV. It's the archetypal foot in the door that will help you create an impression and make them want to meet you face to face. It's sometimes odd to think that the whole of your career may depend on the one or two sides of paper that you write about yourself. Because they are designed to make an impression, don't present a CV that is muddled, scruffy or just plain weird. And it's vitally important when you write your CV always to think about the reader and what they are looking for.

They allow you to tailor your message   The important thing about a CV is to show that you are both **right** for the job and **different** enough to be worth interviewing. This is something that people often don't realise when they are writing their CV.

On the one hand you need to demonstrate in your CV that you understand what the company or organisation is looking for and that you match up closely with the criteria they have set. If you are too wide of the mark you won't stand a chance. You also need to show where you are different or better than the competition – that you have the edge.

People often go wrong by going overboard on showing how different they are. This can lead to zany CVs that simply don't get past the door. So drawing up a CV is about balance and about making sure that you aim your arrows good and true.

CVs are universal   You are never too old or too young to write a CV. Many people leaving school find writing a CV very difficult, because they find it hard to identify what it is about them that is marketable. Many older people who write a CV find it difficult to see the wood for the trees. They have done so many things in their working life that it can seem very difficult to get everything down in just a page or so. People who have had an unconventional life or career can find CVs difficult, because on the surface CVs seem only to cater for people who have walked a straight path.

You will see how to overcome all these anxieties as you work through the week. Put simply, a CV is for *everyone*.

CVs are infinitely adaptable   You decide what to say and how. You don't just fill in the boxes on someone else's form. In fact CVs are as adaptable as you and your own circumstances need them to be.

One very important point is that the CV is not just your chance to talk about what you have done at work. It's also your chance to present other skills and experiences you have picked up during your life. Indeed in some circumstances you can show, through your CV, that your life experiences are more relevant and valuable than your work experiences. All areas of your life and work can be brought to bear – but sparingly and tightly focused on the job you are applying for. So a CV allows you to select the appropriate parts and leave out the interesting but irrelevant bits.

Where are you starting from?
Of course, where you are starting from and what you are aiming for will have an impact on your CV. So you may be any one of the following – and more than one at different times:

- You may be a school leaver with the problem that you have very similar qualifications and education to other people. The challenge in this case is to look at ways of adding value and showing how you are different, and how your experiences inside and outside of school actually mark you apart from your peers. So in your CV you might stress the clubs you have been involved in, for instance.

- You may be moving on from one job to another job in the field. In this case your CV is an opportunity for you to show that you have the capacity to move up a gear from where you are. So your CV may well be slanted towards presenting your experience and showing why you are capable of making the leap to the next level.

- You may be out of a job, having been made redundant. In this case your CV is your opportunity to get started again. This means you will be looking to show the ways in which your work experience is still valid in the workplace today and looking at any other attributes you have built up in your life that will help you get back into the job market. Take heart, there are routes back!

- You may have taken early retirement or be an older person. In this case you will probably have a whole host of life skills that you can draw on and experience that you will be able to present in your CV. It may also be an opportunity for you to show that you're still in touch with the job you are looking for, and to cash in on your most bankable asset – your experience.

- You may be a returner to the job market, having looked after or cared for relatives or brought up children. It's often tempting to think you are at a great disadvantage against all those people with a clear progression to show. However, your CV is an opportunity to stress all the valuable life skills that being a carer gives you, like budgeting, time management and negotiation with benefit agencies and schools. You may also have been involved in voluntary work, helping on the PTA or working in one of the care charities, for example.

• You may decide you want to make a career change. In this case your CV is your opportunity to identify transferable skills that will allow you to move between one career and another.

So, it's important to be aware of all these points before you start working on your CV. All too often people simply plunge in without any preparation or clear idea of the context a CV operates in. What you have done so far today will help you see how your CV is grounded within the general world of selection and recruitment.

Ask yourself:

• What do I want from a CV?
Be clear about the specific results you want it to achieve.

See the wood and the trees

The first step when drawing up your CV is to make sure
you see both the wood and the trees, the detail and the big
picture. This is probably the most difficult thing about
putting a CV together. All of us have had experiences, all of
us have lived lives. The hard part is to give an overall
impression and at the same time to pick out the important
bits that might get us that vital interview.

For many people the effort and discipline needed to pick out
the key points makes them put their CV to the very bottom
of their list of priorities. The best way to counter this is to
have a more structured approach to take the pain out of it.
The first step is to come up with the answers to some very
simple questions. Try these for starters:

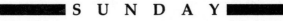

- What three things you have done are you most proud of?
- What three things are you good at?
- What three things are you not so good at?
- What are three personal and professional landmarks in your life?

When you have written the answers to these big questions, think about other things that are important to you, like:

- What kind of job do you really want?
- What kind of things wouldn't you do (for instance, relocate)?
- What kind of work environment do you like best?
- Are you the kind of person who likes responsibility?
- Where and why were you most productive over the last five or ten years?
- If you are meeting a total stranger, how would you describe yourself to them?

You can go on and make other questions up. The aim of this is to start unblocking your thinking and start seeing yourself in a positive way. It should also help you to start sifting through what is important to you and some of your achievements. Unfortunately, a lot of people find answering some of these questions extremely hard.

Be realistic
It's a characteristic of many people that they hate boasting. They're much happier telling other people what they are bad at than what they feel they are really good at.

Go away and boast

A consultant running a seminar on stress management told the twenty participants to go off in pairs and to tell each other what they did better than most (or all) other people. They had to honestly believe their claims and be able to demonstrate their validity through some sort of evidence.

After five minutes, six of the pairs came back. They said they simply couldn't do it. It was embarrassing and wrong to say good things about themselves. However, as the consultant pointed out, if the individuals didn't explain their strengths to other people, who else would? Who else knew more about them than they did themselves?

In other words, being honest about yourself is not the same as being boastful. If a succession of bosses and people reporting to you have told you you're a brilliant communicator, why not share this with the world?.. Suitably phrased, of course.

The best CVs have only the most crucial and relevant details selected. By asking yourself some straightforward questions like these, and giving honest answers, you can:

- Start the process of sifting out what is likely to be important
- Clarify the kind of things you are likely to want on your CV
- Get down on paper some ideas about yourself.

In many ways this should have helped you break the ice and start the process of more structurally putting a CV together.

And finally today

Finally, today is the day to start digging out all the bits and pieces you are likely to need as you go about drawing up your CV during the week. This will help you to feel fully prepared when you come to put pen to paper.

So, get together a pack or pile of all the documents you think might be relevant. These could include:

- Certificates from your formal education
- Proof of training courses you have been on
- Articles you have written
- Addresses and phone numbers of your potential referees
- Any testimonials written by people about you.

Basically you need to get together anything you think might help you, or jog your memory, or that you might refer to in your CV.

Summary

Today you have:

- Clarified what CVs do and why they matter to you
- Thought about yourself and your main achievements
- Got together the bits and pieces to help draw up your CV.

Getting the basics right

Before you start putting detailed information together, it's worth looking at what makes a successful CV in most people's eyes. Then you can put your details into a framework you know is a good one.

There are a number of basic things to get right for your CV to pass the acid test. There's no point in beating about the bush with these. They really are as simple as they seem.

Anyone who has ever advertised a job will have come across CVs that include either all or some of the basic faults we talk about today. They crop up with depressing regularity – ask anyone who has read a lot of CVs.

Before we look at this guide it's important to remember that you are trying to make an impact with your CV. You are trying to show that you are worth interviewing. First impressions count, so you need to make your CV stand out, and not for the wrong reasons.

If you don't do the basics right then it is a case of Do Not Pass Go. Your CV will be filed in the bin.

So what should you do?

Be yourself

One of the things people often do wrong with CVs is try to invent a persona for themselves that doesn't really ring true.

Obviously you want to stress the good things that you have done and stress your skills. But you want to ensure that you can talk about everything you write about. Don't use long words or phrases that, when you are questioned, show you can't really explain them. Try to use language you would normally use and feel comfortable with.

An example

A manager, talking about a CV he had received, said the person had written:

I enjoy working in a synergistic environment.

'None of us knew what she was talking about and we suspected it was a case of using a word she felt would impress without understanding it herself. The phrase clashed with every other sentence in the CV and made me feel uncomfortable with the applicant. On almost that one sentence alone, I chose not to interview.'

Sometimes the CV agencies, who draw up a CV for individuals, write them in a language that doesn't feel comfortable for the person concerned. This sticks out a mile, and it's well worth taking the time to write your own CV. It may not be as standard as the kind of thing an agency churns out, but because of that you have all the more chance of getting an interview. And anyway, it's unlikely that the company will actually believe you are a part-time brain surgeon or heavyweight boxing champion.

And one final thing, try never to copy or adapt someone else's CV, even one you see in a book on *How to write a CV*. Be yourself!

Read the ad

We'll look at this in detail on Wednesday. All too often people don't read the ad properly. They spend about one minute reading the ad and then two days putting the CV together. Their CV may be great, but because they haven't read the advert properly they miss the main points.

> I advertised a job for communications officer at the place where I work. You would be surprised how many people just didn't read the advert and what we were looking for. We actually got one CV in from someone who was a telecommunications worker. He was an

ex-BT person and had seen the word 'communications' in the title and thought the job was for a telephone engineer!

Housing Association Manager

Another trap people fall into is sending a CV whenever they see a job they are interested in, even if the advert doesn't ask for one. This may make you feel better but it won't get you a job.

Often people just have a scatter-gun approach, sending CVs to any jobs they like the look of and not bothering to fill in application forms. If you do this, you will not get an interview, and it's just a waste of another first class stamp. It looks lazy and companies will not take any notice of you.

Be positive but don't lie

This goes back to being yourself, and being honest. On a CV it's important not to pretend or tell lies. If you lie it could give you serious legal problems later on and you may lose your job. What's more, you are unlikely to feel comfortable if you get an interview because you will be worried about being found out.

Length is important

It's important to get the right length for your CV. In general, the shorter the CV the better. Certainly you don't want to go over two pages in length, except for some very senior posts.

The received wisdom is that you should aim for a one page *resumé* type CV that gets all the basic points and leaves the person advertising the job wanting to ask you more.

The act of getting all the major points in about yourself briefly and succinctly is an important discipline. If you find your CV has crept up to more than two pages then get to work editing the sentences and cutting everything that is not relevant to the job. The best way of doing this is to check your CV carefully against the person specification for the job. We look at this later.

Broadly you may say that there are views on the right length of CV depending on the different types of job:

- For analytical-type jobs – like banking or accountancy or anything to do with figures – try to get everything on to one page. For this kind of job you want to appear to be well organised, concise and clear thinking. If your CV for this kind of job goes on to two or three pages it may look as though you can't see the wood for the trees.

- More creative-type jobs. In this kind of job you may well go to two pages because you may want to give a fuller picture of yourself.

- If you are sending in a speculative CV to a company when they have not advertised a job, never write more than one page. Your task is to whet their appetite and encourage them to either contact you, remember you next time or keep your CV on file.

As well as these areas there are other areas to take into account. If you fail any of the following you will not pass go.

Don't use gimmicks

In the past some people who have advised on CVs have stressed the need to be different. This has led to people sending in gimmicky and jokey CVs.

We have seen CVs that have come in on luminous paper, on transparencies, with elaborate shading, that include cartoons, that have been headed by family photographs and that are on paper sizes other than A4. One person sent in his CV for the job of swimming pool manager on the back of a pair of flippers!

These kind of CVs are very unlikely to impress. During the 1980s in a very small section of the market – advertising and so on – this kind of wacky approach to CVs was the norm. However, as recession has bitten, and organisations have started to take their business a little more seriously, it is almost bound to turn people off. Keep your CV personal, engaging and professional.

Another tip is, never try to be funny. Your idea of humour is likely to be peculiar to you. One man wrote in his CV under *Educational Qualifications*:

I was the original exam nightmare – I threw up before every exam!

What he meant was that he had no qualifications.

The nuts and bolts

The following is a checklist for getting the nuts and bolts right:

- The CV must be clean and tidy. It shouldn't be creased or have ink blots. Above all, avoid the dreaded white correction fluid. If you are still using a typewriter make sure you type absolutely perfectly. The mere sign of a white patch covering a mistake will probably guarantee your CV a future in a rubbish bin. Organisations produce quality paperwork these days, so yours has to match their standard or they'll almost certainly reject it.

Join the 20th century, please!

The real advice here is to get hold of a personal computer (PC), even if you have to go to someone's house to use it. You really should be using a PC these days. PCs allow you to store standard paragraphs, move things around, change them, print them out, and generally rework and develop your CV.

If you have got a PC you can store things and develop your CV over time. So try and find a way to bin your typewriter and join the 20th century.

- The layout must be clear and neat. There are varying opinions about how much margin to leave, but avoid cramped or crowded pages. It's important not to suddenly reinvent yourself as an ace designer and use 15 typefaces and various avant-garde type designs. Keep it simple, keep it professional. Remember that headings are important but don't go overboard. Above all, don't try to do anything too fancy, especially with typefaces.

- Spelling and grammar are crucial. We know of people who have won jobs on the basis that they knew how to spell, and could tell the difference between *principal* and *principle.* It's absolutely essential that you avoid spelling mistakes and grammatical errors. If necessary, get someone else to check it before you send it.

  If you are not good at spelling, use the spell check on your PC, but don't rely on it. You may type a word wrongly but still not be alerted to it by the spell check – for instance you may type 'spell' as 'sell' and because both are correct the computer will let it go.

- Only handwrite the CV if the company insists on it, and then use black ink rather than blue. It photocopies better and makes their life easier. If you are going to use handwriting, be aware that some employers use handwriting analysts. If you send a handwritten covering letter or envelope, take time with your writing, and make sure it's neat.

- Politically correct terminology can matter. Some organisations have moved into the realms of political correctness, and, if it's important for the employer, you need to make sure that this is reflected in your CV.

- Keep something back. CVs often fail because of sheer overload. People become so exuberant and carried away with themselves that they put every possible fact and detail on their CV. It's very important to keep something back, so that you can talk about it at the interview and possibly surprise your interviewers. In the CV world less is definitely more.

Summary

Today you have looked at some of the basics of putting a CV together. If you get these right you will have at least jumped the first hurdle. And when you have jumped the first hurdle you can go on to tomorrow, which looks in more detail at researching what needs to go into the ideal CV.

Avoiding the pitfalls of CVs means avoiding the obvious things like spelling mistakes and poor grammar. Make the CV look neat, tidy and professional. There are also some slightly less obvious things like the importance of being yourself and using language that suits you.

If you get these things right you should be able to build on today and put together a CV that really works.

Knowing you...

Today you start doing some research on the company you plan to send your CV to. All too often, advice on preparing CVs tends to concentrate just on the piece of paper you come up with. However, it is preparation and research that allow you to draw up a cracking CV, one that will work for you. This avoids the common problem of CVs being drawn up without a specific context.

At the end of today you will be able to take a firm decision about whether the job and the company is right for you. If it isn't, you'll save yourself the price of a first class stamp, and possibly some heartaches too.

> *Computers*
>
> Remember, with today's modern computers you can save text and edit it and move it around. This means you can keep key paragraphs and re-use them, tailoring your CV to the company without having to type a whole new one each time.

There is no excuse for not doing your research on the company. Companies are likely to take more interest in you if you take the time to demonstrate an interest in them.

But there is another reason why it's worth researching the company or organisation you are thinking of sending your CV to. You may decide after you have done your research that you do not in fact want to work for them. There is no point in sending a CV and possibly getting invited to an interview for a job that isn't really right for you.

Reading job adverts

It's important to realise that there is often a great deal below the surface of a job than meets the eye. To be effective with CVs you must get to the real truth. The following rules should help you to start reading job adverts so you can decide whether or not to go for the job, and if you do, to tailor your CV to fit.

In a job advertisement, there are two levels to be aware of:

- The **surface level**. In other words there is a whole range of basic things you need to make sure you match up with, like the qualifications that are asked for and so on.

- **Below the surface**. The important thing with adverts is to do a kind of Sherlock Holmes exercise and do some detective work. When you read a job ad you need to ask questions like:

  - What does it really mean?
  - What kind of person are they really looking for?
  - What kind of work environment is it really likely to be?
  - Is this the job for me?

So, look at what the advert does say, and what it doesn't, and then make a judgement. A large part of tailoring a CV is to make sure your language and style matches up with the employer's language and style. You can pick up lots and lots of clues from the job advert about the kind of culture in the organisation.

The following is a beginners' guide to reading job ads. We will then look at a couple of actual job ads and see what you could find out from them to help tailor your CV.

A guide to job ads

- What are the buzz words? Use a highlighter pen and pick out any particular buzz words that seem to relate to this company. Lots of companies use a kind of shorthand that means they are looking for a certain kind of person. If they mention self-starter or self-motivator for instance, the chances are they want people who don't need a lot of managing.

- Ask yourself whether this is the kind of place you are looking to work at. What is the job ad hiding? Is there anything behind the wording that might point to something rather difficult or unpleasant? Have they left things out that you would expect to find? For instance, does the advert fail to mention salary, or that it is an equal opportunities employer, when all similar jobs mention this prominently?

- More to the point, if you know your job market well, is this job in character with it? If it isn't, beware! It may mean the company hasn't thought through the job properly and is confused about what kind of person they want.

- Ask yourself what can you learn from the style of the advert to help your CV? And, of course, will the culture of the job really suit me?

So, although it sounds obvious to say, 'read the advert', it really is important to study it carefully, both at the superficial level and below the surface.

Some job adverts

Look at the following job advertisements. The technique you'll use is one you can apply to all advertised vacancies, so it's worth trying it out a couple of times.

The Fabulous Group

Come and join one of Birmingham's fastest growing companies. We are dynamic and innovative, and based in brand-new, high-tech offices in the heart of Birmingham. We are currently wanting to recruit a part-time receptionist (hours 9.30 – 12.00).

We want a well-presented, enthusiastic and experienced person to help in the busy atmosphere of our front-of-house reception. You need top-class communication skills and to be super confident in liaising with clients. You will need to show a flexible approach and be able to work without supervision.

Please write in confidence, enclosing your current CV with a daytime telephone number to:

Mr Scottish Claymore, The Fabulous Group, Pinkerston House, 1 Victoria Square, Birmingham.

The Fabulous Group employs over 1,000 staff.

Search for clues

What does this job ad really tell us about the company? For a start, what kind of qualifications are they looking for? What kind of skills do they want?

When you have done this kind of exercise you can start to decide whether you actually have the skills and mapping them out in your CV. Apart from the obvious things like excellent communication skills which the advert asks for, what else is there behind the ad?

Something to do

Write down what you think the company will be like, and what you think the job will be like.

What do you think they will be looking for from a CV?

There are lot of interesting things about this advert, including the words *dynamic* and *innovative* early on. It's probably a lively and rapidly changing company, unlikely to be particularly bureaucratic. You need to ask yourself if you would like to work in this kind of environment, where companies can grow rapidly and decline just as fast, or whether you would be happier in a settled place. The choice depends on you.

The advert also asks for a well-presented person, so you need to be smart, clean and tidy. It may also mean that the company is obsessed with image, and if you aren't this kind of person the job could be wrong for you.

The job is part-time, and you need to ask if you would be happy with this, especially as it seems they are looking for a high level of responsibility. Some people want part-time jobs because they aren't highly responsible, and you need to make a decision here.

The company is a large local employer – this is useful because you might start to do some research to find out more about the company.

The whole advert stresses the importance of confidence and enthusiasm. It's a front-line post dealing with lots of enquiries and people. It may well involve dealing with irate clients and problems. Again, you need to ask yourself whether this is the kind of place you want to work.

Finally, you need to work without supervision, so you might have to solve most problems yourself. You need to ask yourself whether you could cope with this kind of job, or whether you would thrive in this kind of atmosphere.

So, if you decided to go for it, your CV would need to stress your:

- Self-reliance
- Ability to manage yourself
- Dynamic and independent nature
- Ability to get things done and to deal with people.

A different kind of job

Senior Youth Worker

Coronation Youth Centre, The Borough of Swaffham

£20,000 - £23,000

We need a person who will be at the forefront of developing a new style of youth work at our centre. We are located within the northern wards which are part of a council-wide development. You will need to be adept at following council policy and developing the Council Equal Opportunities Policy too. You must have a recognised JNC qualification plus two years' full-time experience, or four years' experience as a full-time youth worker.

You must have the ability to plan and deliver a programme of youth work and work with council officers to make sure the council policies are delivered effectively.

We offer a casual car allowance and car loan facilities.

We are an Equal Opportunities employer and we welcome applicants from all sectors of the community. Disabled people meeting the job requirements are guaranteed an interview. Employees are not permitted to smoke at work. We have a work-based nursery.

A question

What does this tell you about the job and the organisation?

This advert tells you masses about the job. For a start, you need a range of experiences and qualifications to get past the first hurdle, and qualifications and experience come pretty near the top, so the employer obviously thinks they are important. You would need to stress these areas early in your CV, to stand a good chance of getting an interview. However, there are lots more clues to pick up in this advert.

There are two references to council policy. The chances are it's a relatively bureaucratic organisation and it's likely you will be quite closely supervised by your political masters. There is more than one reference to equal opportunities, and you need to decide how much this reflects the ideology of this particular council. You need to be in sympathy with this approach, or at least accept it, to apply for this job. If you are very anti-equal opportunities or like getting on with the job on your own, this is not the job for you.

Finding out more

If you can, try to find out more about the company, to help you tailor your CV to fit. There are lots of avenues for doing this, and it's worth putting some time in.

The following check-list gives some ways of finding out more about the company you might be sending your CV to:

- Companies will send you annual reports, prospectuses and customer information leaflets – but watch the delivery time if you're up against a deadline. Documents like these can give valuable insights into what the company thinks and the way it works. You may even find from the documents that you have done work in a similar kind of area, and this can only help your cause and strengthen your CV. Staff magazines are also good because they give you a better idea of the company culture and the way it operates. In fact, some staff magazines tell you more than almost anything else, certainly about the atmosphere and what the place is like to work in.

- The public library keeps directories on business and the public sector. These are often split into areas of interest, for instance media, retail, finance and so on. In these directories you will find details of what the business is, where it operates, and its size. Ask the librarian and check the reference section. You can also visit specialist libraries like the City Business Library in London, which has lots more in-depth detail about companies.

- The media is a good source. Check all local press coverage and you may well find stories about local employers that can help you again to tailor your CV. On the other hand you may well find references to problems which may make you think twice. You may also find stories about recruitment drives and community involvement which could help you shape your CV.

- Every trade or profession produces specialist magazines aimed at people working in that trade or profession already. Again, the library can help here. These can make quite interesting reading and they can certainly give you a way of finding out more about a particular company, or at the very least about the sector.

• Don't forget the informal network: friends, relatives and contacts through your leisure activities and hobbies can give you a great insight into local employers. Someone who already works there can give you a lot of low-down on the kind of place it is to work. These people can also help you to tailor your CV to the way they think will help get you that all-important interview.

Red light or green?

So, what's it to be? Will you go on and do a CV for this company? Or will you decide the job and the company are not for you after all?

Summary

One thing that should have come through clearly today is that what you write needs to match what the person advertising is looking for. We haven't said, 'if they say they want someone with a driving licence, tell them you've got one', because you know that matters. What we have said is that you need to stand back, think and research before starting to put down the details. Once you have the big picture it is relatively simple to see the shape and fill in the details.

You have looked at the importance of reading job adverts in great detail and looking above and below the surface, to find out as much as you can about the job.

You have also looked at ways of doing research into organisations to find out more about them. Armed with these two crucial elements you can go about creating a CV that is tailor-made. It also shows that you have thought about the company. It's this kind of thing that can really help you get an interview.

Anyway, even if you don't get this particular job, if another job comes up in the sector, none of your research will have been wasted. In the CV game you get out what you put in. Tomorrow you are going to get down to the business of starting to write your CV.

Knowing me...

Today gets the ball really rolling for your CV. After all the CV is about you. It's your way of saying something about yourself that will get you that all-important interview. It is also a job that requires selection and judgement. You can't write everything about yourself – save that for your best-selling autobiography. On the other hand you can't write a CV in a two-line telegram.

Yesterday we gave you several clues for linking your work experience to the requirements of the company – matching your experience to what they see as important. Today you'll look at yourself more broadly, and choose a format for the CV that fits the company and you.

A useful technique for getting a clear picture about yourself is called retrieval mapping.

Retrieval mapping

The idea behind retrieval mapping is actually quite simple. Retrieval mapping is a technique for pulling out or retrieving key experiences you have had and skills you have built up, that you can then use to help develop your CV. Follow the simple, step-by-step guide below to your own retrieval mapping process.

Step 1: division
Divide your life up into significant blocks that you can concentrate on. This will allow you to focus on different parts of your life rather than see the whole thing as a jumble. It is an organising tool.

The kind of divisions you might come up with are things like: school days, late teens, twenty to thirty, thirty to forty, forty to fifty, fifty plus; or school, university, early jobs, management jobs, senior management jobs; or school, and outside school. It's up to you to divide the cake in whatever way you think would be most helpful.

The key is to give yourself manageable chunks that you can actually focus on, and then think about what you did, what you learned, and what skills you developed during that period.

Step 2: blocks
Write on a large piece of paper one block that you have identified above. You may want to have different pieces of paper for each of the different blocks you have identified.

Step 3: arrows and bubbles and things
Now place the block in the middle of the page and draw lines or bubbles or arrows from it, linking everything you did that you thought was interesting or you learned something from.

Step 4: patterns and shapes

When you have done this for each of the blocks put them all on the table in front of you. You can now start looking for patterns and common areas between the blocks. As you look through you might want to use a highlighter pen and highlight every time when similar responsibilities came your way.

You may start seeing a pattern in things like:

- You've often worked with teams
- You've often led teams
- You have a consistent pattern of doing administrative jobs and enjoying them.

The choice is yours, but what this activity will show you is where there has been a repeatable pattern of events throughout your working and other life.

So you should be able to highlight:

- Your skills
- Your experiences
- Your achievements.

You can use these in your CV. You may also start identifying highlights that you definitely want to talk about. Flag these up using a different coloured pen.

Drawing the picture

This is a simple example of what we mean, done by a woman who has a wide range of experience in each of the blocks she picked out. The one shown here is for the *school* block.

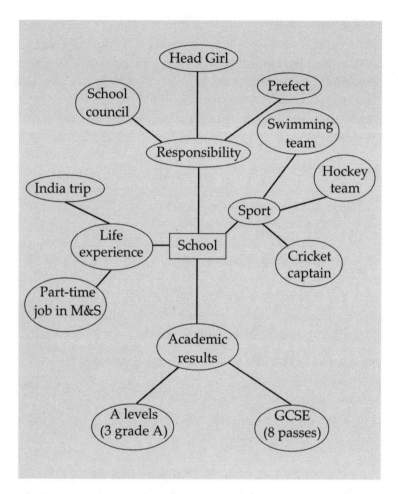

Drawing the conclusions
The following shows the results of this individual's retrieval mapping, putting the blocks together. She has condensed the information into what she feels are the key points to make it manageable.

School
Head Girl
Cricket captain (not usual in girls' school, then)
3 A levels, grade A
Travel to India

University
Degree
Amateur dramatics
Edited university newspaper
Travel to Indonesia

Early 20s
Researched report on lawyers
Cricket captain
Worked as researcher and team leader

Conclusions
There is a pattern of:

- leadership
- an enjoyment of physical activity
- thinking work
- a broadness – reflected by the travelling.

So, now you know what the company wants and what you have to offer, it's a question of sorting out the best format for the specific circumstances.

Choosing a format

One of the beauties of CVs is that you can construct them in a way that best suits your purposes. This means you are not stuck with a standard format that might not actually suit you.

The key today is to think about some of the different kinds of format, and then select one that will do the job you are looking for.

The basic formats

It is important not to feel that choosing your format is a complicated or technical affair. In fact the choices are quite simple and the advantages and disadvantages of each are straightforward too.

> There are two basic formats of any CV. These are:
>
> • Chronological
> • Functional

There are some other options as well, like going for a completely free-form approach, or tailoring your CV specifically for one job. We won't look at these in detail because these are on the extremes of CV writing. Instead we will concentrate on the two major areas, and look at the benefits and problems associated with each. By the end of the day you will be able to choose which suits you best, and helps you to get that job.

The chronological CV

As the title would suggest, the chronological CV starts with your most recent job, and then works backwards. This format gives your most recent job the most space and emphasis. Commonly in this kind of CV you will see that the title of the organisation is prominently displayed. A chronological CV may look something like this:

1990 – present

First Offer Housing Association

Development manager. Managing development projects and putting together funding bids. Preparing spreadsheets for management committee. Managing a team of three development officers. Handling a budget of £500,000.

1985 – 1990

Dyfed Community Housing Trust

Development officer. Project managed building projects on site. Carried out regular financial audits of the department. Set up tenants liaison group.

The case for   The advantages of this chronological format for a CV is that it emphasises the continuity and the way your career has grown gradually and progressively over time. It also allows you to bring out the names of employers which may in turn help you get an interview.

If I see a CV from a person who has worked for one particular company, I automatically give them consideration because I know the excellent training they offer. Everyone who's good has basically worked for that company at some time.

Personnel Manager

Another real advantage of this format is that it is very easy to follow – after all it follows a simple order.

So this kind of CV is best when you have had a pretty clear career direction, and you can paint a straight-line picture. It's also good if you have worked for some well-known employers.

The advantages also include:

- Showing you have worked in the same field for a number of years
- Helping to establish continuity which may be important in more traditional employment areas.

And against   The disadvantages of this kind of approach are obvious. If you have had a career history that is a little patchy, then it can be difficult to do this chronological type of CV. This is because the gaps tend to show up clearly.

This kind of CV is also difficult if you have had a career change and decided to retrain in a completely different direction at some point.

In today's market people often change jobs quickly, and this has meant that the chronological CV has become less and less useful. If you have to list six or seven recent employers it can make you look flighty.

Another problem with this kind of approach is that it can highlight if you have been in a job for a very long time – which might make you look like a stick-in-the-mud – and of course it also highlights when you have had a big career break.

Finally, this kind of CV is no good if you are fresh into the job market. It emphasises your lack of work experience – and may make you seem lightweight.

The functional CV
This is the alternative to the chronological CV and gives you the option of presenting a view of your main skills areas. The following is an example of a functional CV for a restaurant supervisor.

Peter Flemming
56 Flightborn Road
Persham
Middlesex UB5 7QT

Staff Management

Supervising 12 staff during busy shifts. Carrying out appraisals. Organising rota system. Running the team rewards system.

Budgetary Control

Controlling and managing a budget for the restaurant of £180,000. Checking time sheets and authorising expenditures. Presenting financial report to management each month.

Customer Care

Dealing with any customer complaints. Setting up and running customer care training programme for team members.

The benefits   Looking at this CV you can see the real benefits of this approach. For a start it allows you to be clear about the skills you are able to offer and the areas in which you have worked. The actual titles of your jobs and your work history are in a more secondary position. This approach adds focus.

The advantages of this are that it can give you great flexibility and allow you to avoid repeating yourself as often happens in a chronological CV with many similar jobs.

This kind of CV also overcomes the fact that you have not had a lot of experience at work. The emphasis on your functional skills and experience allows you to blur some boundaries and smooth over some of the gaps – after all in this kind of CV you are not emphasising progression.

You may also want to use this approach if you are looking to make a career change because it allows you to emphasise transferable skills that will help you make the transition. By the same token you can use the functional approach if you are returning to the job market after a gap. You just present what you learned during the gap.

The problems This kind of CV isn't useful if you want to emphasise continuity and growth, and it may not be right for more traditional jobs. Many jobs want to see a progression up the career ladder.

If you take this approach it might also mean you lose the impact of any prestigious companies you may have worked for.

Working on the words

The final thing you will do today is think through some of the words you will use when you come to look at your work history tomorrow.

All too often CVs are written in a rather limp, non-committal way, using phrases like 'my duties include', 'I have been involved in'.

What's more, the act of putting together a CV is sometimes seen as a glorified administration job – with you simply pulling together lots of existing material and slapping it down on a piece of paper. Not true.

Instead you should see putting your CV together as a writing job. It is a job where you need to work hard on the words and choose them carefully – after all, you only have limited space to get the message across. So every word counts!

Using active words
The main way to get away from a rather flat delivery is to use active words to describe your skills, experience and achievements.

Active words allow you to concentrate on the results you have achieved and present them in a focused and up-beat way.

The following is a prompt list that should help you. Each word in the list is the kind of positive action word you can use when drawing up your CV. They help impress a potential employer and really bring home to the full what you do.

Achieve	Create	Manage
Analyse	Develop	Organise
Capable	Economical	Process
Consistent	Expand	Sell
Control	Guide	Specialise
Coach	Improve	Train
Co-ordinate	Lead	Wide background in

Something to do

- Add some positive words of your own
- Now write some sentences describing your skills, experience and achievements using these words.

Summary

Today you have reflected on your strengths in some depth and some different options for CVs. You have looked at retrieval mapping and at two approaches, chronological and functional, to preparing your CV. In addition you looked at the use of positive words when describing your work history.

Put together, these should help you tomorrow when you come to putting together the first version of your CV.

Getting down to the writing

Today you are going to get down to the nitty gritty of writing your CV. You might think it odd that you have waited so long before you actually start the writing process, but being prepared is important.

With the preparation you have done, the writing should come easy and you should be able to get it right first time. Of course you will want to come back and edit your CV, checking it for spelling, grammar and punctuation, but the point is that all the preparation should help you see clearly, and it is this that makes a good CV. It's in the thinking and planning that a tip top CV is made.

So you have chosen your model, you've had a think about the style and some of the words you are going to use. You have also done a retrieval mapping exercise where you have dredged up the most important things in your life and career and then started to look for patterns. So now it's time to get to it. You can't put it off any longer.

Over the next two days you will write your CV.

Thinking through the sections

There are many different ways of doing this, but it's important to be clear about some of the sections which you might use in a CV. This means stopping and thinking before writing it down.

Put yourself in their place

The most powerful way of structuring the sections and the content of your CV is to pretend you are reading it for the first time. Put yourself in the position of the person you're sending it to and make a short list of the most important factors you'd be looking for. If you can step into their shoes you will be able to really choose information that is relevant to them. You don't want to bore them or turn them off.

It's hard work

The manager of a large furniture department in a chain store says that she sometimes gets over 100 CVs for fairly junior management posts. The first thing she does is scan the CV and within four or five seconds makes a decision whether it goes on the 'A' pile (the desk) or the 'B' pile (the bin). It's as tough as that and her advice is to make sure that what you write is going to seem immediately relevant to her.

In other words, think it through and put yourself in their shoes – write what they want to read, not what you want to write.

There are probably as many differing views on which sections and what information should come where, as there are managers reading the CV. We will look at these a little later. The important thing is to be aware of what the basic sections are likely to be in any CV. Then you can decide on the order and the emphasis to suit your situation.

A model you can use

1 Personal details

This section will include your name, address and other details personal to you.

2 Education

There is some debate about whether this should come early in a CV, or towards the end, although the more experience you have, the further towards the end of the CV it should come. Here you put the names of your schools and colleges and the qualifications and training you have received.

3 Employment

This is the crux of any CV. It is where you carefully match your working life against the demands of the job you are applying for. In fact, you have already done substantial preparation for this section through:

- the initial retrieval mapping exercise

- thinking through the right format for you

- choosing power words to describe what you have done.

Packing it in or packing it together

If you had 17 jobs in selling during the early years of your career, don't list them all. It is too long and too boring, and it could give the false impression you don't stick at anything.

Think about grouping together early experiences that aren't individually exciting and making something more chunky out of them, like:

Between 1982 and 1990 I built up considerable experience in sales, marketing and management with national and local firms in the electronics and food processing sector.

4 Interests

All too often this goes horribly wrong for people, or at the very least you can miss an opportunity to impress. The interests section is your chance to show that you are a rounded human being and to show how interesting you are.

Cricket captain

The retrieval mapping you looked at earlier showed a woman who had been cricket captain. The interest in sport was demonstrated by the other activities as well, but having been cricket captain in a girls' school is something that will grab the attention of employers and make the CV stand out from many others.

5 Extra information

This is your chance to put in anything that doesn't fit well elsewhere and paint a picture of some of the skills you have. You can also use this section to say why you are interested in the type of work you are applying for.

Getting it wrong

The job of a Careers Officer can involve helping students compile CVs and identify their strengths and weaknesses. One CV from an applicant for a Careers Officer post said, under the heading 'Additional Information':

My father is a Principal Careers Officer.

That's all it said. As an example of terrible role modelling for the job it was classic. The individual was not interviewed.

6 References

This section speaks for itself. It is where you give the names and addresses and phone numbers of the people you have asked to give you a reference.

Would you mind...

Notice the words above – 'people you *have* asked to give you a reference'. NEVER put someone's name down and then try and contact them to tell them you've done it. For a start, it's simple bad manners and anyway, it could go radically wrong. If they feel annoyed at being taken for granted, or are now going to have to give a reference but they don't actually rate you as much as you thought, the results for you could be negative.

What to do today?

Because we are taking a step-by-step approach, today you are going to look at the first couple of parts of this broad model.

A thought

The important thing with a CV is to try and stress the unusual and present information about yourself that will impress the reader. People often include details of any travelling they have done on a CV for this reason. Your travels can often be an interesting way of presenting yourself as an individual.

However, it is important not to go mad and stress too many zany things about yourself. If you are an expert in colonic irrigation, our recommendation is that you keep it to yourself.

Personal details

This section is straightforward, but it's important to start with some don'ts before we get on to the dos.

Where people often get this section wrong is to put too much detail in. So, don't give details of:

- Your weight
- Your age
- Your place of birth
- Your next of kin

- Your National Insurance Number
- Your health
- Your marital status and whether you have any children (especially if you are a woman because this may be used to discriminate against you).

Sadly, in the ageist society we live in it is not advisable to put in your date of birth if you are over 40.

The layout in this section

All too often this personal details section also becomes stilted.

One of the problems here is that people run text down the left-hand side of the page in the following way:

Name: Peter Morris
Address: 54 Orchard Close
            London
            W6 3BR
Telephone: 0181 634 7252

This starts your CV on a highly formal and uncomfortable way. Much more effective is simply writing your name and details like this:

Peter Morris
54 Orchard Close
London
W6 3BR
0181 634 7252

If you want to add any more details about yourself, why not add them to the additional information section. Using this section also allows you to get quickly to a real hook – either your education or your work experience.

By presenting your name in this human and straightforward fashion you have made a statement about yourself. It also allows you to be slightly less formal with your CV whilst still being professional and getting all the important information in.

There are a few options in this section. If you think it would help you get the job, you could also mention whether you have a clean driving licence, for instance.

Remember though, you don't want to take up too much space with this section, and you want to make a crisp start with your CV and get onto the stuff that will get you that all-important interview.

Education
The debate is where to put your education. Maybe the simplest answer is to decide how important the person reading the CV will think it is. If you have been Managing Director of a multi-national company, maybe your seven GCE 'O' level passes aren't that crucial?

Traditional CV advisers have always stressed that education should come up front in a CV. However, the more experienced you are the more likely you are to relegate your education to almost the last item on your CV.

Of course, if you are just leaving school or college then your education is very important and it should be at the beginning of your CV. The judgement on this is really yours.

The main problems people have with putting together their education sections are:

- how much detail to put in about the education
- how to set this section out.

The detail

In this section don't be shy to put all your qualifications at school. You don't need to give the grades for GCSEs if you went on to do 'A' levels. Don't give details of exams you failed.

The key here is to put down all the qualifications you have, because it's likely to impress. You may then want to add a separate section where you list your training.

All too often people tend to downgrade the value of training, but to many employers the training you have received is every bit or even more important than your formal education. After all, the employers who trained you thought it was important enough to spend money on, so why shouldn't other employers?

So put down here every training course you have attended and any certificates you have. Today's modern organisation values training, so use this opportunity to tell them about what courses you have done.

Do try to leave out irrelevant certificates and awards like the fact you earned a fire-lighting badge in the scouts or passed your cycling proficiency test.

The layout

This section often looks messy because people are left with a large block of text with both their place of education and their qualifications. A way of counteracting this is to break the section up into easily definable chunks.

So, you might have a section headed *Places of education*, which lists the schools or colleges you went to, and where they are. Don't mention your primary school here.

You can then have a separate section headed *Qualifications*. Again, contrary to normal advice, we think a good idea is to start with the most recent qualifications you have. So if you have a degree, start with it and then work backwards.

Summary

Today has seen you start the CV proper. You have looked at the sequence and content of the early sections from the perspective of the person reading it.

Tomorrow you'll finish it off.

Almost there

It's Friday, and you're almost there with your CV. You have put a lot of work into getting the first draft of some of the key parts of your CV, and now it's time to round it off. But remember, when you have rounded it off, you still need to go back and check it carefully. Make sure it does the job you want it to and that the spelling, punctuation and grammar are correct. Attention to detail is all-important.

You've done personal details and education, so on to the next part.

Work experience

This is vital and it is here that your CV will either succeed or fail. There are a number of key things to bear in mind when you write this section.

Keep it relevant
Many jobs these days will send out a person and job specification and you can use this to match your work experience section with what the job requires and the person to do it.

So go through the job and person specification and pull out all the:

- special skills – the things you really need to be able to show you can do and

- experience – the areas you need to have worked in over the years

that are needed.

Write these down on a sheet of paper or highlight them in the specs.

Then for each, write down your skills and experience to match. If you find you do not have a perfect match with your work experience you may be able to match using things you have done or learned outside work.

Working through the specs in this way will help you put only the relevant details into your CV. Don't put in things that seem interesting just for the sake of it.

Show what you have done…
… rather than simply tell. For instance rather than telling the reader:

I am computer literate,

show that you are computer literate:

I am an advanced user of Lotus 123 and have designed integrated spreadsheets. I have a good knowledge of Word for Windows and a basic knowledge of the database programme Delta 5.

Remember to use those power words we looked at earlier. But always keep it concise and to the point and keep on matching your CV with the person and job spec. If a company goes to the trouble of putting together a person spec, then they will use it. So don't ignore it.

Don't be put off
Be realistic but don't be too easily put off. If the specification asks for five years senior management experience for instance and you only have three, don't be too put off. Often companies are prepared to bend the rules.

However if it asks for five years experience and you only have five months worth, then it probably isn't worth making the application. You will need the skills of a professional magician to conjure up this job and present a convincing CV.

What's in a name?
It is important to think through what job titles you want to use on your CV. Very often, organisations give you job titles that in no way reflect what you actually do.

The following list shows some of the job titles you might want to consider:

- Accounts Manager
- Customer Services Manager
- Clerical Manager
- Carpenter
- Managing Editor
- Development Officer
- Executive
- Press Officer
- Operations Manager
- Printer

and the list goes on.

If you have opted for a functional CV then you might also want to spend some time thinking about the functional headings you can use to group your ideas under.

The following are just some possibilities:

- Advertising
- Banking
- Budgeting
- Communications
- Entertainment
- Managing
- Problem-solving
- Team building
- Supervising

and so on.

Expanding on your personal skills

You need to pick up on your personal skills. All too often people are shy or coy about their personal skills.

The following is a check-list of some of the personal skills you may be able to identify in yourself and then use.

Expanding your list of personal skills

The following are just a few of the personal skills you may identify. Have a look and see whether there are any on the list you could claim for yourself.

advising people	handling projects
arranging events	inspecting quality
calculating numerical data	interviewing people
checking for accuracy	managing resources
coaching people	motivating people
compiling figures	operating equipment
co-ordinating events	persuading others
counselling people	planning agendas
dealing with difficult people	preparing charts
delegating responsibility	raising funds
drawing up plans	reviewing
editing documents	running meetings
selling products	supervising staff
setting up demonstrations	teaching
speaking in public	writing reports

Now add any of your own to the list.

You should try to get as many of these personal skills as possible into this work history section. And remember, always link them with action words if you can.

Smoothing over the years
All the research shows that very few people list all their experience down to the last month. Often they gloss over a gap or two or the odd dreadful and short experience by adding a couple of months to the previous job and bringing forward the start date for the next one. We're not telling you to lie, obviously, just telling you what the research says.

If you have had career gaps, career changes, or are returning to work, you may choose the option of going for a functional CV to help smooth over the years. However, one other way of doing it is to list your jobs in terms of years not months. This will allow you to cover up any gaps you have. The other option here is to be up front and honest about any career breaks you have had. You may well do something like this:

Career break 1991 – 1993.

I took a career break to look after my mother. During this time I used my time management skills, and further developed my negotiating skills with the local authority and medical agencies.

Other tips for this section are not to put down why you left a job, and not to mention the salary you were receiving.

Are you interesting?

What you need to tackle in the next section is your interests.

All too often these are a lost opportunity for people.

For instance, if you just put down that you like reading and walking the dog, you won't look like a very interesting person. You are likely to rank somewhere below Steve Davis in the 'interesting' stakes. So, make a list of all the different things you might list as interests. This could include being involved in sport, the arts, or running clubs. The trick is to give a balanced, portfolio approach to your interests. Putting down that you like playing cricket, rugby and football may make you look a bit light on the old grey matter.

One of the tricks with 'interests' is that you must be honest. Don't put down that you have a lifelong fascination with pop music if you wouldn't know your David Bowie from your George Michael.

As you write down your interests, think through what the employer is looking for as well. Try and work out why what you write could matter to them. If it's a job that involves lots of management you might decide to highlight an interest that reinforces this, for instance putting on a production at the local amateur dramatics society, rather than just acting in it.

The key is to make yourself look like a lively and well-balanced person. You need to show you have a life outside work, and how you believe your interests will actually help you do the job you are applying for.

The following prompt list might help:

About your spare time activities

The following prompts might help you construct an interesting Interests section. Leisure activities are given alongside ideas showing why they might be relevant. These are just ideas and aren't the only possibilities by any means.

Possible leisure activities

- Painting — creative, calm
- Mountain climbing — achieving, fit
- Playing a musical instrument — creative, achieving
- Woodwork — creative, practical
- Keeping fit — good health at work
- Golf — competitive, active
- Bird-watching — dedication, research
- Watching live music — artistic, relaxed
- Cycling — fitness, self-managing
- Motor racing — enthusiasm, technical

Possible social activities

The chances are a prospective employer will want you to have some kind of social life even if they work you too hard to have one for very long. Involvement in the following examples of social activities can demonstrate a range of personal qualities, including most of those listed above, as well as a willingness to work with others and put something into the system.

- Parent-teacher association
- Drama group
- Choir
- Sports team
- Youth club leader
- Voluntary work
- Photography club

Extra information

This is the section where you can give a broader picture of some of the skills you have and maybe why you want the job as well. You can also tailor it to fit the job you are applying for.

For instance, if you were applying for a job in housing, then this is where you would mention that you do some voluntary work for *Crisis at Christmas*. This will allow you to add credibility to your application and show you care about the field you are applying for.

This kind of section is particularly important if you have gaps to deal with in your CV and you feel you haven't dealt with them adequately in the rest of your CV. This is where you may be able to explain the gap, and show what you got from the experience.

You can also write here if you have travelled, or indeed anything that has taken you away from the normal steady progress of a career and adds relevant interest to your CV.

In this section you can also put other key skills and experiences you think might help you, like owning a car, having a clean driving licence, being a qualified first aider.

When you write this section you usually write it in full – in an informative and friendly style. For instance:

In my spare time I produce the community news letter. I write and edit it and design it on an Apple Mac computer using Microsoft Word 5.1. I then organise for it to be distributed around my local streets.

So it's here you can pick out something interesting that may just be the difference between getting an interview and not getting an interview. And it is the winning edge you are looking for.

Personal achievements

Even Rab C Nesbitt probably has some personal achievements – so don't be afraid to mention yours.

Many people add a short section to their CV outlining their main achievements and responsibilities. This is another way of using power words and of focusing in on important aspects of what you have done – but this time away from work.

It can be hard to think through your personal achievements – often because we find it difficult to value the things we do.

You can use the following check-list to help you. Of course, it isn't an exhaustive list – it just gives you a flavour of the kind of things you may have achieved.

Personal achievements

You may have built up any of the following achievements:

- been elected an officer in a club
- managed or coached a sports team
- played a role in a drama group
- been awarded a medal
- made a rescue attempt

- climbed Snowdon
- completed a marathon
- made a film
- gained a certificate for study
- been a prefect at school
- had an article published
- gained a Duke of Edinburgh award
- learned a language
- gained any award, honour, decoration, prize or distinction.

References

Only this section to go and you're there. There are some golden rules for references, which are:

- Choose people who are going to give you a good reference – take no risks.

- Ensure you contact your referees first, to make sure they are happy to act as such for you.

- Make sure they are available when they need to be. There is nothing worse than choosing referees who have headed off on a round-the-world trip just at the time you need their backing.

- Choose referees who know enough about you to give a real insight into your personality and strengths. Don't use people you only know fleetingly.

- Choose referees – especially character ones – who have a good job of their own. This could help add weight to their reference.

- Include the telephone numbers of all your referees in case the person who is advertising the job wants to ring them.

Choosing suitable referees

The following are just some of the people you may consider as referees. They give your CV some authority and some weight.

- Bank Manager
- Head Teacher
- Manager or Ex-Manager
- Personnel or Ex-Personnel Officer
- Supervisor or Ex-Supervisor
- Magistrate
- Teacher
- Tutor
- Doctor
- Councillor
- Lecturer
- Church Warden
- Minister
- Chartered Accountant
- Justice of the Peace
- Solicitor
- Local Government Officer

Some of the books on CVs say that you should not actually put your referees in your CV and instead that you should write:

References on request.

There doesn't appear to be a good reason for doing this... unless you know better. Choose references who you are happy to have on your CV and, if it is difficult for these people to be contacted before you are interviewed, then make it clear to the company advertising the job that they can contact them after your interview. It can only help your application.

If you have a poisonous boss who you think will not give you a good reference then don't use them. Instead, choose someone else at work who does know what you are made of to act as your referee.

Summary

Today you finished putting together the first draft of your CV. You looked at how to handle the remaining sections and have ended up with enough material to make a decent job of it. It might need a bit of polishing, but you're nearly ready to send it off.

That's for tomorrow.

Getting your CV across to the employer

Today you look at presenting your CV and completing the task of getting it to the employer.

Presenting your CV

We have already touched on this but it's very important to get the presentation right.

Remember that first impressions count and if your CV looks messy, cramped, confused, complicated or massive then you won't get very far with it.

There are some pretty simple dos and don'ts when it comes to layout.

- **Do** make your CV look professional (try to produce it on a PC and print it out on a laser printer).

- **Do** keep it simple (avoid using lots of typefaces or too much underlining or emboldened text).

- **Do** keep the layout easy to follow and understand (keep a reasonable margin down the left-hand side of the page, use simple blocks of text and make sure the columns are justified – this means that the text lines up in one block).

- **Do** have plenty of white space (plenty of space makes a CV easy to read and an appealing prospect too).

- **Don't** get overcomplicated and try to prepare a masterpiece of modern design with your CV, unless, of course, you are a designer.

- **Don't** cram everything on to one page if it doesn't fit easily (go onto a second page rather than cram everything onto one page).

- **Do** use clear headings on your CV. If you opt for a functional CV then choose your headings with care. They should be short and clear and punchy.

- **Do** use bullet points (this list is an example of bullet points). Bullet points allow you to pull out the punchy bits and separate your ideas clearly. They look good and professional on the page and they help people to pick out what is important.

This is how you might use headings and bullets to make your CV look good:

Jane Stevens
87 Wildwater Drive
Norwich
Norfolk
NR12 7TY

Sales • Managed three retail outlets in Norfolk

• Coached departmental managers

• Increased turnover by 50%

• Set up staff training system and appraisal system

Writing that letter

When you send your CV in, the chances are you are going to write a letter in with it as well. The important thing is to keep the letter simple and professional while still giving a flavour of your unique personality.

In the letter be clear about what you want to achieve from it. Your letter should:

- include a reference to the job you are applying for

- be brief. The person already knows quite a lot from your CV – if you ramble on in the letter, you will detract from your CV and may create a negative image

- be polite and courteous

- be positive but not too cocky. Avoid sign off phrases like:

  You must see me tomorrow in order to help your company get the competitive edge it needs

- be without spelling mistakes and be neatly typed or hand-written.

It's a letter not a book

One person who advertised a job and asked applicants for a CV and letter reports the following:

I advertised a manager's job. One person sent a good CV, but the letter was a horror. It went on for 5 $\frac{1}{2}$ pages and just rambled. The person just threw everything in hoping something would stick.

The job itself required the manager to draw up reports and think clearly. I felt that the letter I received threw doubt on the applicant's ability to do this so I decided not to interview them.

You might also use your letter to pull out one or two interesting points that relate to you and the job. It's also here that you might be able to show some of the research you did earlier. For instance, you might be able to make reference to a new factory the company has opened or an exciting new opportunity you have read about.

Here is an example of a letter. Notice that it's written in a personal and informative style and does enough to whet the employer's appetite without throwing in lots of unnecessary detail.

Dear Mr Claymore

The Post: Clerical Assistant

I enclose my CV in response to your advertisement in *The Morning Echo* for the job of Clerical Assistant.

As you can see from my CV I have five years experience of clerical work. I have completed a number of training courses, and have a computer at home that I use regularly.

I was interested to read about the way your company is expanding in the local newspaper. I would like to be a part of your forward-thinking and exciting organisation. I enjoy working as part of a team and thrive on meeting tight deadlines.

Feel free to contact any of my references, or indeed to phone me or write to me at home.

Yours sincerely

Jane Greene

Nearly there
You should now have a CV that is virtually ready to be sent. All it needs now are a few last touches... and a stamp.

The finishing touches

You have done all the hard work, and it's now just a case of getting everything ready to go.

Take time to check
The first thing to do is read everything through just one more time. If you have been working hard on your CV over the week it can often be difficult to pick up any errors that have crept in.

Basically, everyone sometimes gets a bit too close to their own work, so today give your draft CV to an understanding friend, or your partner, and ask them to read it through carefully. The chances are they may well spot the odd mistake or give you suggestions before you finally type it up. If they do, say 'thank you very much', make the changes and then print the CV out again. It will also pay you to give your CV one more read just to see if you can improve it.

Remember though, don't start fiddling with it if it is already good. With any writing there is a law of diminishing returns. You get your work to a stage you are happy with, and then any further work does not actually improve it enough to warrant the extra time spent.

Written or typed letters
So you've got your CV and you've worked out your letter. You now have to decide whether to handwrite your letter and give it a more personal touch or whether to type it. This is a decision for you to make, and will be based on your judgement of what the people will be looking for. It shouldn't be one that costs you sleep.

A handwritten letter:

- has the personal touch
- feels more intimate.

But if your handwriting is poor then it will not do you any favours.

A typed letter:

- is more professional but less personal.

When you have got everything together, put it into an envelope, and write the address neatly on the front. Stick on a first class stamp and post your CV.

You've done it. Now it's time to wait and see whether you have got that vital foot in the door to help you get the job you want.

One final clue

You have seen us stress the importance of seeing the CV process from the other person's perspective, so, if you feel brave enough, ring them up and ask them what they thought of your CV, should you get a polite refusal.

You have absolutely nothing to lose and you could pick up some really helpful information that you can use next time.

Looking back over the week

Having completed your CV it's worth looking back and recognising how it all came together.

On **Sunday** you looked at why CVs matter and what they are. You explored the fact that they work for everyone, but they need a fresh approach sometimes to reflect specific situations.

Monday was the day you looked at the nuts and bolts – what makes a sound CV in terms of length, style and so on. You looked at the need for any CV to be positive and in the right language.

On **Tuesday** we took you through the steps of analysing the receiver's needs – what the person you're sending your CV to is looking for. This helps you target your approach and makes what you did on **Wednesday** more focused. Remember, Wednesday was when you looked at retrieval mapping and reflected on yourself.

Thursday and **Friday** were spent sorting out the sequence and the content of your CV, so that they made sense to the receiver and on **Saturday** you tidied it up, added the accompanying letter and sent it winging on its way.

Further *Successful Business in a Week* **titles from Hodder & Stoughton and the Institute of Management all at £6.99**

All Hodder & Stoughton books are available from your local bookshop or can be ordered direct from the publisher. Just tick the titles you want and fill in the form below. Prices and availability subject to change without notice.

To: Hodder & Stoughton Ltd, Cash Sales Department, Bookpoint, 39 Milton Park, Abingdon, Oxon, OX14 4TD. If you have a credit card you may order by telephone – 01235 400414.

E-mail address: orders@bookpoint.co.uk

Please enclose a cheque or postal order made payable to Bookpoint Ltd to the value of the cover price and allow the following for postage and packaging:

UK & BFPO: £1.00 for the first book, 50p for the second book and 30p for each additional book ordered up to a maximum charge of £3.00.

OVERSEAS & EIRE: £2.00 for the first book, £1.00 for the second book and 50p for each additional book.

Name: ....

Address: ....

....

If you would prefer to pay by credit card, please complete:

Please debit my Visa/Mastercard/Diner's Card/American Express (delete as appropriate) card no:

☐ ☐ ☐ ☐ ☐ ☐ ☐ ☐ ☐ ☐ ☐ ☐ ☐ ☐ ☐ ☐

Signature .... Expiry Date ....